C000253912

DESIGN SOURCES FOR PATTERN

Jan Messent

Contents

Introduction and Definitions of Pattern Types   Page   3

Natural/Organic Pattern   4

Structured Patterns   5

Planned Pattern   6

Combined Patterns   7

Observing and Recording   8

Ancient and Primitive Patterns   12

Strips and Stripes   15

Distorted Lines   16

Interlaced Lines   18

Squares   20

Triangles   24

Circles   26

Connecting Circles   28

Moving Circles   29

Spirals   30

Scallops, Shells and Scales   32

Animal Patterns   33

Flowers and Foliage   34

Foliage Borders   37

Border Patterns   38

INTRODUCTION

No book, however comprehensive, can hope to cover all the ground in a search for pattern; examples are far too numerous and diverse. In forty pages, one can only hope to be introduced to the basic elements, to methods of looking, seeing and recording and then to develop a nodding acquaintance with the various forms, styles and possibilities as they have been exploited by man throughout the ages.

In a source book of this kind, it is tempting to include a collection of decorative motifs which are the stuff of which many patterns are made, but until one understands *how* to construct patterns, these would be of little use, except as single motifs. Instead, I have included only those which are themselves examples of repeating elements and which therefore qualify as pattern just as they are, for the keyword to understanding pattern is "repetition". To say how many times a unit must be repeated in order to qualify as pattern is not easy to answer. A symmetrical pattern consists only of two halves, one of which is an exact mirror-image of the other, and yet a simpler unit (an apple, for instance), may have to strive much harder (a whole row, perhaps) before it will have the impact of a pattern. Nevertheless, examples are to be found all around us, indeed our whole lives are bound up in one huge cosmic pattern of repeated days, weeks, movements and rituals, like dance, music and poetry.

Pattern appears accidentally in footprints on sand, snow or mud, and as tyre-tracks; we stir cream into a drink and make a pattern of swirling lines, or we decorate a cake with a random pattern of icing. It is often static as on the carving round a doorway, but is just as often moving as in a pattern of clouds, or ripples behind a boat. To many of us, patterns are so familiar that we scarcely recognise them at all, the greengrocer's stall of fruit and vegetables, the yarn shop with its racks of coloured yarns, bookshops, clothes shops, all are patterned with colour, texture, size and shape. Even the ordinary washing hanging on the line makes a pattern of shapes and spaces.

The following pages form a kind of notebook of pattern ideas taken from the ordinary world of an ordinary person. Everything shown is, in one form or another, available for attention and inspection by anyone with the curiosity to search and the designer's need to gather raw material. Having become familiarised with pattern in its many forms, the reader can then take on the role of pattern-maker using the other book in the series, "Designing with Pattern" (ISBN 1 874080 65 8) which explains many of the construction methods and ways of translating design material into patterns.

Definitions of pattern appear to fall into the following categories,

Natural/Organic Pattern. Patterns under this heading are usually formed by some form of growth, life and the elements. They are found in such things as reflections, foliage, strata and animal skins, shells and microscopic organisms. Pebbles and soap bubbles are composed of small units repeated in large quantities, these being roughly the same shape though not necessarily the same size. However, the fact that they are repeated in close formation makes a random pattern of an organic nature.

Structural Pattern. This is a term used for patterns which emerge automatically out of the materials and techniques used by craftsmen, for instance, builders, weavers, basket-makers and boat-builders. The primary purpose here is not to construct a pattern but to build or make something safe, strong and functional, however, long use of the materials has proved that the best methods also, by coincidence, produce a pattern. Patterns of a more elaborate nature may be incorporated into the product for added interest and beauty, but never at the expense of the functional capabilities unless the item is purely for decorative purposes. Obvious examples of structured patterns appear on buildings in brickwork, stones, tiles, beams and so on. Textile artists build patterns into their weaving, knitting, crochet and lace merely by constructing a plain piece of fabric.

Planned Pattern. The function of patterns commonly known as "ornament" or "decoration" is solely to make more beautiful, or interesting, something which already exists. The repeating units chosen by the designer may be borrowed from any source, but the essential quality here is that the repeating elements are planned, plotted and designed in advance of the final technique, either on paper or in the mind. Some planned patterns are so elemental that they can be produced simultaneously with the work without preparation. Some complex patterns have been memorised by skilled craftsmen, and others must be plotted in the utmost detail to be programmed into a machine or worked by hand. Methods vary according to the material, method of production, and complexity of design, but planned patterns are, because of the possible permutations of so many elements, techniques and media, limitless in variety.

Combination Patterns. Where any of the three previous categories overlap, combination patterns occur. Examples of this are not hard to find; shadows of tiny leaves on a patterned wall, a row of apples on a striped tablecloth, the broken image of a row of trees seen through a wire fence. This is one of the most fascinating areas of discovery as examples tend to be unexpected and visually exciting, making excellent design material for all techniques.

Whilst these four categories form the basis of the explorations in this small book, other examples prove more difficult to define. How does pattern differ from texture?

In simple (perhaps over-simple) terms, pattern is recognised primarily by sight, and texture by touch. However, the area of overlap (and confusion) exists because it is also possible to recognise some patterns by feeling at them (the cables on an Aran sweater, for instance) where the pattern is in relief. These bear the extra definition of "textured patterns" and are common to craftspeople who work in textured and sculpted materials. It is also possible to recognise some textures simply by looking at them because our previous experience and our powers of deduction give us strong clues about the way in which they might respond to our touch without our actually doing so. Any baby animal must learn this by touching everything, often with the extra-sensitive lips. Never-the-less the first explanation remains true, that one can always *see* a pattern though one may not always be able to feel it. Similarly, one can always feel texture (even smoothness is a texture) though it is more difficult (and unreliable) to discover its tactile qualities just by looking at it.

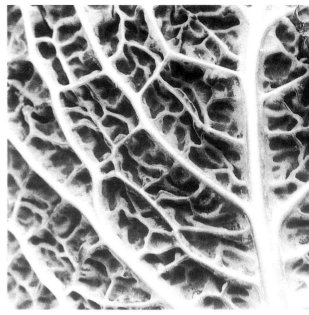

[Above : photo courtesy of Gene Sparks.]

Natural/organic pattern can be seen in the twisting lines of a tree, the ridged underside of a cabbage-leaf, the ripples of sand along the sea-shore, and the markings on the skins of snakes.

Although quite different in origin, there are distinct similarities in some of the patterns shown here.

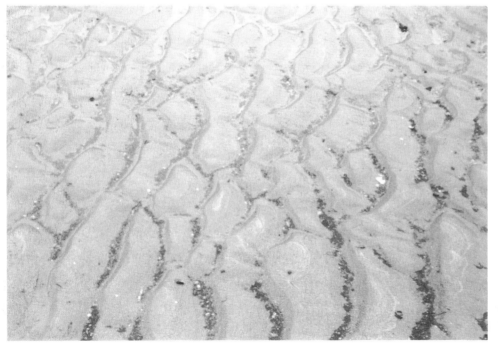

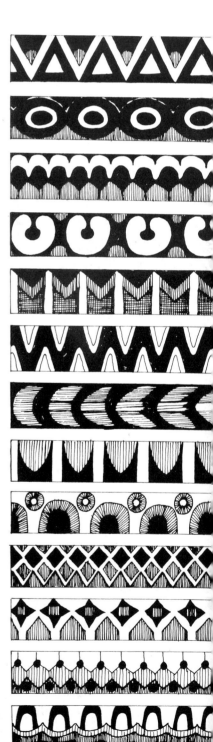

Structured patterns are sometimes formed by coincidence — as in the sawn-off ends of stacked logs — and partly by planning — as in the well-known brick chimneys of Hampton Court Palace. Still, the essential element in the pattern is the material itself. More structural patterns can be seen in handwritten and printed words, especially newsprint with its variety of type-faces, and in music, where symbols and lines dance in rhythm across the page. Weaving and basketry are favourite sources of structured pattern as are all kinds of builders' materials, even though an element of planning can also be observed. Other textile techniques such as lace, knitting and crochet all have inbuilt pattern, and, in the latter examples, this applies even on plain single-stitch pieces as well as on planned designs.

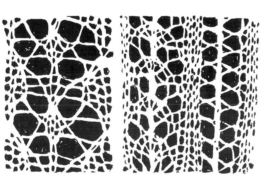

bdfhkltdbfhkltbd
OXOXOX
JANJANJ
SCSCSCS
gjpqygjpqygjpqy

Planned Pattern

The designer of an old 19th C. applique quilt used four units, arranged inside a square, to make a BLOCK. The square block now becomes a unit which is repeated enough times to make a large quilt. Many planned patterns are based on a framework known as a GRID which ensures that the units and blocks are arranged accurately and in the correct order as decided by the designer.

The panels of this Romany caravan were used as a grid to assist the placing of the carved and painted motifs on the front and sides, and the face of a Maori warrior was the grid used by the artist who tattooed this symmetrical spiral pattern. A chart used by a knitter is a form of grid, and manufacturers of wall-paper, printed fabrics and patterned floor coverings base their designs on grids too.

However, not all planned patterns require grids: there are other more informal ways of planning which are used by many glass engravers, sculptors, wood-carvers, jewellers and ceramicists.

6

Combined Patterns

Below: the patterned surface of Christmas paper has been cut by scissors to create another pattern of negative shapes. Cutting folded patterned paper is more interesting than using plain paper because patterns are then interrupted in an unforseen way. Try this out on stripes or on your own painted patterns.

...ve: sunlight filtering through net curtains (structured/ ...nned pattern) shows through the fine leaves of a house- ...nt, giving the impression of traditional blackwork embroidery. ...the same time, the formality of the lace pattern is broken ...e and there by the density of the foliage. The various ...es caused by this effect are more interesting than ...us of straight unbroken pattern.

Bottom left: blackened sandstone capitals form a purely decorative (planned) pattern of foliage on this already interesting structural pattern of stone blocks: a fascinating combination of units which, because of its familiarity, may be quite overlooked as a potential source of design.

Below: a spring hedgerow (organic pattern of lines), seen through a wire mesh fence (structural pattern) dripping with raindrops provides an intriguing mixture of images which tempts one to cut up the picture along the wire lines and separate the rectangles by tiny recessed spaces with raindrops hanging in front.

Observing and Recording

Designing is about seeing, recording, adapting and re-arranging visual material gathered from every possible source. No special sight-seeing or fact-finding missions are required for this; our own environment is full of potential material if only we can learn how to recognise it. Examples of pattern are closer than you think: take a sketch-book around your home, workplace or garden and make rough sketches like the ones on the opposite page. These are the elements of pattern and your sketching is an exercise in observation. Don't ask yourself what you are supposed to do with it at this stage, just be happy to discover an example, observe it, look closely enough to draw it and then keep your examples as reference. Exercises like this are an essential part of a designer's preparation, mentally and physically, and everyday practise will result in a file of ideas and a more perceptive method of observation. Your drawings are merely reminders, not for general consumption, nor for approval, but for your eyes only.

Look at repeated shapes and lines.

Look at the negative spaces between shapes.

Carry a small lightweight camera about with you. Black and white film is just as useful as colour film, sometimes more so, as the results highlight pattern, texture and tonal relationships without the intrusion of colours.

Use an optical kaleidoscope to give you more pattern awareness. This will remind you of constructions and shape combinations. Doodle patterns on squared and isometric paper.

Be aware of pattern caused by shadows which change according to the light source at different times of the day.

Keep photographs and cuttings of pattern examples in an album, scrap-book or filed in a shoe-box for easy reference.

Pattern in Living

Apart from the patterns seen in our environment, the idea of pattern extends into other forms, probably the most significant of these being the patterns of life itself. Birth and death, renewal, fruition and decay, the seasons, tides, patterns of time and habit, behavioural patterns. Some of these examples lend themselves well to visual interpretations, while others are more abstract.

More patterns can be found in

Poetry - sounds, rhythm of syllables, formation of verses.

Music - notation symbols, sounds in small or larger sequences, the formation and arrangement of choirs and orchestras.

Dance - more specific group formations which change with the music, repeated movements and rhythms. Folk dance, tribal dances; costumes add to the basic patterns.

Games - outdoor (rather like dance) bodies make patterns of coloured clothes, lines and groups in similar movements. Indoor patterns of chequered boards and other markings, moving pieces and component parts, dice, cards and other graphics.

Word Associations - thinking about a subject on all levels, not only the more obvious visual links, often produces a new wave of ideas for creating and using pattern in a more meaningful way. Use Roget's "Thesaurus" to help you find more associated words, for example:

rhythm, arrange, repeat, structure, organise, sort, regiment, order, adjust, compose, select, counterpoint, balance, interval, space.

A collection of associated words will sometimes bring to mind a visual connection: an image which can be well expressed in terms of abstract pattern instead of by more conventional pictorial means.

The art of many primitive societies shows how this has been done since earliest times, and the symbolism expressed in pattern can be found in ancient cultures as far-flung as those in North America, China and Central Europe.

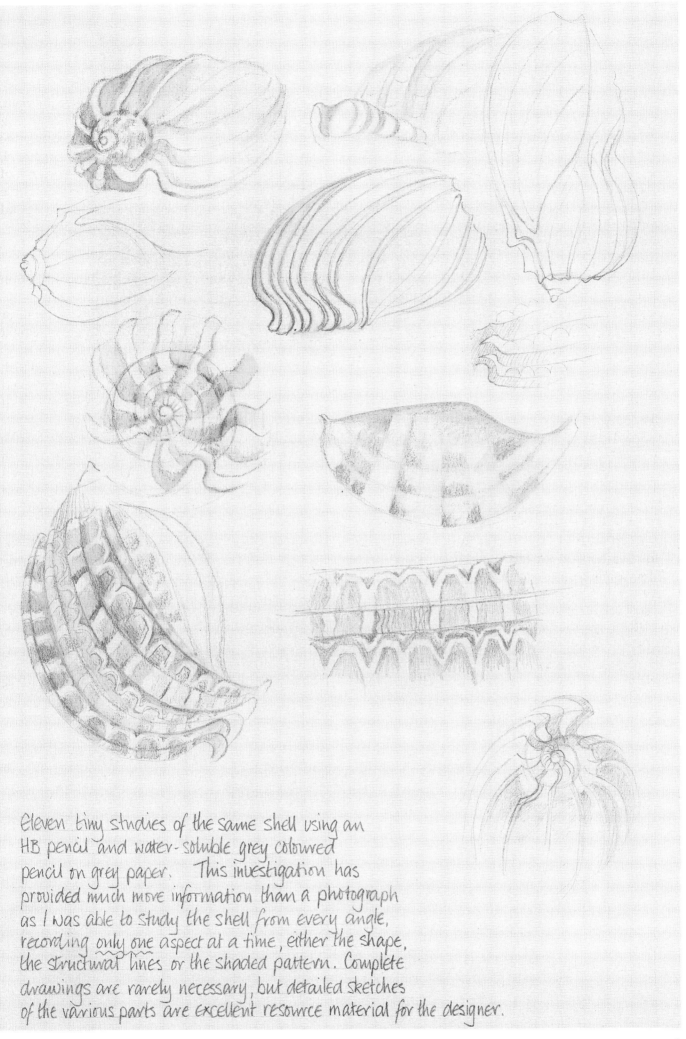

Eleven tiny studies of the same shell using an
HB pencil and water-soluble grey coloured
pencil on grey paper. This investigation has
provided much more information than a photograph
as I was able to study the shell from every angle,
recording only one aspect at a time, either the shape,
the structural lines or the shaded pattern. Complete
drawings are rarely necessary, but detailed sketches
of the various parts are excellent resource material for the designer.

Examples of pattern in the environment may be seen as formal structures, like the building opposite, or as informal arrangements like these chairs and table. But, leaving aside their function, designers tend to see things as pattern-objects and habitually explore the spaces <u>between</u> shapes, as seen in the sketch below. These negative spaces are not "left-overs" but are just as much part of the pattern/design as the more positive shapes which are seen at first glance. They can be changed into the positive element of a pattern during the experimental phases of designing.

Cut a circle of about 2½" (6 cms.) diameter from a piece of plain paper and enclose any part of this sketch inside it, to find an abstract pattern of shapes and lines. Turn the sketch sideways and upside-down for more arrangements.

 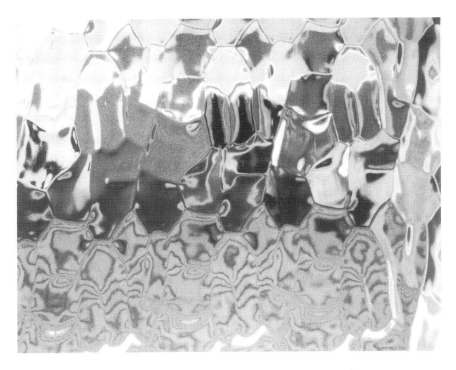

Allow the eye to remain a little longer in exploration before moving on to new ground. This can lead to the most unexpected and rewarding visual material. The patterned glass in a kitchen door changes its proportion of tones as objects move on the other side of it. A camera helps to fix these tones and catches the effect of watered silk in connected bubbles of shape.

A closer look at the windows in this New York sky-scraper reveals that each one contains an amazing pattern of lines and swirls which reflect the glass windows facing it. The camera catches this effect more easily and instantly than a sketch because the strain on the eyes at such a distance can become tiring. The resulting patterns make excellent material for quilters. Some of the blocks would link together, and separate blocks could be made to re-assemble in a variety of arrangements.

This small panel is a pencil-drawn reconstruction of a Coptic tapestry of the 4th— 5th C. Now in the Victoria and Albert Museum, London, it illustrates how a simple border of flower-heads has been used by ancient weavers to such good effect. At one time, this may have been part of a garment, needle-woven into the weft threads as the rest of the fabric was being woven on the form. Notice how, of the fourteen flower heads, three of them are different, one of these completely so. This discrepancy (for what reason, I wonder?) makes the border all the more attractive, and suggests that complete uniformity in the repetition of motifs is not necessarily a top priority.

Artefacts dating back thousands of years show that man has used pattern as decoration in the same ways it is used today, on pottery, in carved relief, weaving and wall decoration.

The figure on the left is a plaque from Marrão in Portugal and dates from between 2000–3000 B.C. The steep triangles are similar to the decoration (below) found on a bronze vessel from Hungary dating from the seventh century B.C. The harpist on the right of the design plays to her companions who weave on a weighted loom and spin with a drop spindle.

The highly-patterned papyrus (right) is a detail from a painted ivory plaque in the centre of the lid of a small chest from ancient Egypt.

Left: a geometric pattern dating from c. 5000–2000 B.C. found on a painted rock at Hinna, Norway. Below left: a repeating pattern from a bandeau made of wool of the Nazca period, Peru. Below right: a clay stamp seal of 5000–3000 B.C. from the Quetta Valley, India. Lines, dots, triangles and squares: these were the main ingredients in the earliest of man's attempts at decoration. They are still commonly used today.

13

Top: decoration on the outside wall of a building in Reading, Berkshire. Lines, cables and blocks in stone and cement.
Bottom left: detail from a piece of Ashanti Kente cloth from Ghana, always woven in narrow strips which are sewn into one large piece of great beauty.

Above: the Austrian artist, Gustav Klimpt (1862-1918), painted some highly decorative figures many of whom wear robes of a strip-patchwork construction. Patterned fabrics are included.

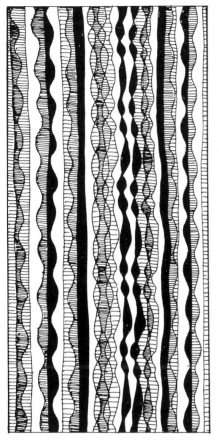

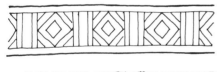

Strips and Stripes

The repetition of lines is one of the earliest and simplest forms of pattern which has been used as a decoration from pre-historic times.

Lines may be repeated rhythmically and in sequence or at random. Many striped patterns have motifs included between the lines; others vary in width and spacing or have their frequency interrupted by over-printed irregular motifs.

Collect samples of striped fabrics, wall and wrapping-papers, and have them photocopied so that they can be used for design experiments without destroying the originals. Cutting up and re-arranging is probably one of the easiest and most successful way of acheiving an immediate result of unusual striped patterns.

Above: the underside of a wooden spiral staircase.

Top left: tapestry-woven bands of wool and nettle fibre. Potawatomi Tribe, Michigan. c.1890

Bottom left: 19th C. Salish blanket of finely twined wool. Puget Sound area. Smithsonian Museum of Nat. Hist.

Centre: detail of a woven belt from Guatemala.

Below: incised pottery decoration by Iroquois Indians, and "doodles" showing how stripes may be cut at an angle and re-positioned horizontally or vertically.

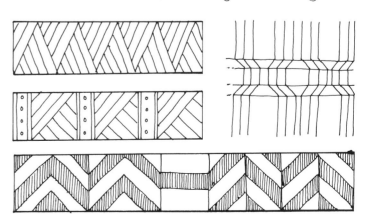

15

Distorted Lines

Wonderful distortions occur when straight lines fall as shadows on to uneven surfaces. Fences, railings and scaffolding give good examples of this, but notice reflections of these in water too. Trees reflected in this way are often distorted even more by the passage of boats and birds. Notice how similar the water patterns are to the wood grain and tree bark patterns looked at sideways.

Look out for more distorted lines in
striped fabric awnings and deckchairs,
wasps' nests,
paintings by Hundertwasser,
coils of rope,
striped animals,
cooked spaghetti,
swirled glass paperweights,
cream swirls on food,
ski-tracks in snow,
paddy-fields,
sand ripples on the beach,
clinker-built boats,
hair styles and
striped upholstery.

Interlaced Lines

It may seem obvious to point out that, once lines begin to cross each other, shapes are formed in the spaces. However, until we have learned to see *every* aspect of the thing we are observing, it is easy to lose sight of this fact in our pre-occupation with the pattern made by the lines. The illustrations show a diversity of examples where lines have been inter-laced and linked to form shapes of two and three dimensions. Some of these also develop into isolated units of design (called MOTIFS) in which the lines are joined to form continuous (un-ending) links. In others, the lines flow in rounded or angled coils to form border patterns, and some of these spring from quite solid sections, as though organically. Indeed there is something positively organic about the Art Nouveau examples which spring directly from the ancient Celtic strapwork designs of coiled mythical animals and plants. Many brilliant and humorous examples of these designs can be seen in the Lindisfarne Gospels and the Book of Kells (see below) and other early Christian manuscripts. The interlaced designs shown here illustrate that these patterns are universal and derive from basic skills as old as the tying of knots in girdles, ribbons, ropes, and in the binding of hair, axe-handles and spear-heads. The knot has deep symbolic significance in many countries and religions which no doubt accounts for its wide use as a decoration in every medium. Many examples of the continuous inter-laced line pattern can be seen on borders of manuscripts, stone and wood-carving, pottery, weaving and carpets. Basketry employs the inter-weaving of lines in its structure and many Japanese printed fabric patterns have evolved directly from this.

The material used in the construction of the article on which the decoration is placed has an immediate bearing on the style: this can clearly be seen in the relatively straight lines which criss-cross each other in basketry and in the angularity of the woven lines on the tapa cloth made of tree-bark fibre. Compare these with the more sinuous lines carved on the back of the stone dragon in Kew Gardens (top of page), the knitted cables of soft yarn and the bendy silver coils of the buckle.

Motifs now begin to emerge which isolate themselves from the more continuous types of pattern seen so far. These motifs may either be used as a single decoration to give emphasis to part of a design or they can be repeated in the same way as any other more simple motif. The following pages show examples of continuous patterns for borders and larger areas, and also of motifs which can themselves be divided up to contain elements of pattern. In this way we can see that pattern fulfils many purposes in a variety of roles, to cover large areas, as borders, as single spot motifs, or as part of more complex free-style designs in a larger context.

Notes on the illustrations overleaf:
   a. and b. Stylized knotted tassel cords from Japanese clothes.
   c. Design on the back of a carved stone lion in Kew Gardens, London.
   d. Japanese motif of interlaced Y shapes.
   e. Tibetan interlaced design. One of the Eight Auspicious Emblems known as The Endless Knot. To the Tibetans, this symbolises love and devotion.
   f. Knitting patterns made by cabling, originally used on fishermen's pullovers, they symbolized ropes and cables.
   g. Design on part of a silver buckle in the Art Nouveau style. Made for Liberty of London in 1899 and known as the "Cymric Style".
   h. Tight curls of false hair on top of a fringe hair-style.
   i. Islamic knot motif carved in stone.
   j. Interlaced design on the haft of a Celtic spear.
   k. Interlaced motif from a tile of the Italian Renaissance.
   l. Design for a candlestick by Rex Silver. 1900 Art Nouveau.
   m. Interlaced border design of Celtic origin.
   n. Design on tapa cloth (made of tree bark) from the Congo, Africa.
   o. Interlaced basket design from Japan.

Useful books for patterns of interlacing:
   Ashley's Book of Knots./Clifford Ashley. Faber
   Celtic Art: The Methods of Construction. George Bain. Constable (London) ISBN 0 09 461830 5
   The Book of Kells./Thames and Hudson ISBN 0 500 27192 5
   The Styles of Ornament. Alexander Speltz. Dover

Mummified cat. Ancient Egypt

a. b. c. d.

e. f.

g. h. i.

j. k. l. m.

n. o.

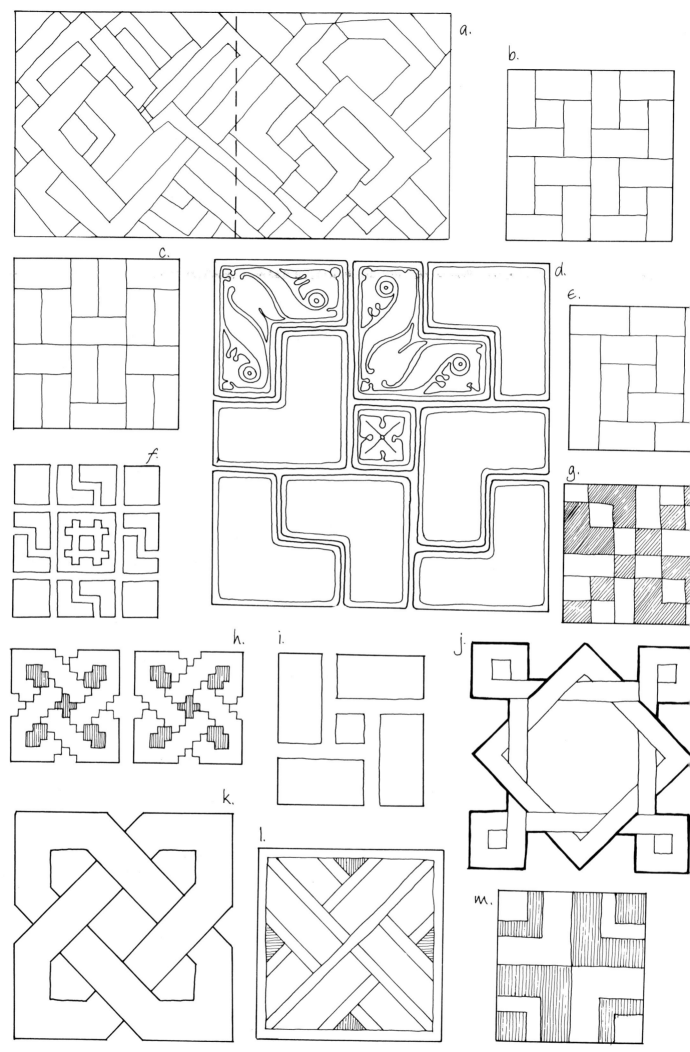

a.

b.

c.

d.

e.

f.

g.

h.

i.

j.

k.

l.

m.

20

Squares

These two pages illustrate squares which have been divided up by straight lines to form more geometric patterns inside them. Several examples follow on from the interlaced patterns of the previous page. This is one of the simplest ways of making patterns with squares, others being to use squares as blocks and build them up to form a larger patchwork, or to make a border, or to overlap them to form more squares where the overlaps occur.

Notes on the illustrations :

a. and g. taken from designs by the Parisian artist Edouard Benedictus. (d. 1930)

b. c. and e. brickwork patterns. Ideas for these are found in gardening and building books.

d. from a tile of the Italian Renaissance.

f. design from an Irish bowl found in a Viking tomb in Norway. See also i.

h. and k. two versions of a simple knotwork motif of Celtic origin.

i. and m. from the author's sketchbook: in its layout, i. is similar to d.

j. Islamic motif carved in stone.

l. design from the back of a garden seat.

n. detail of a design from a poncho of the Inca period (Peru. 16th C.) now in the Cleveland Museum of Art, U.S.A.

o. and q. derived from Islamic tile designs.

p. a small detail of one of Liberty's most popular fabric designs from the Clarion Collection by Susan Collier, 1972.

n.

o.

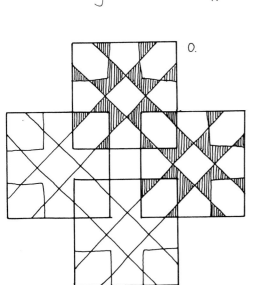

p.

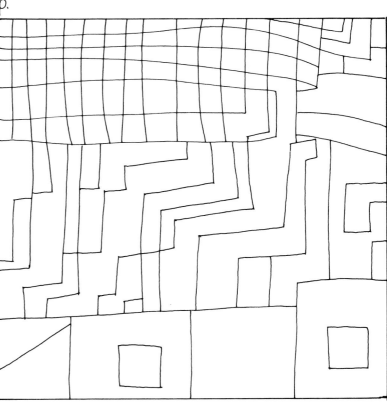

q.

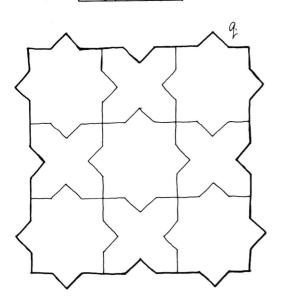

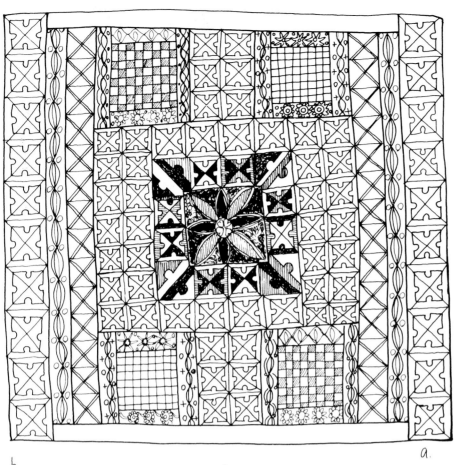

a. Detail from the centre of a patchwork quilt from south-eastern Germany dated 1776-1779. The drawing shows the bare bones of the design which is much more richly patterned than it appears here. The balance of light and shade (just indicated in the centre) is brilliant in its application over such a large and minutely detailed area.

b. Majolica tile of the Art Nouveau period.

c. Stamped print on cotton from the Ashanti people of Ghana.

d. Motif embroidered on a robe from West Africa.

e. Tiles from medieval England.

f. Patchwork motif — "Forbidden Fruit."

g. Tree branch doodle.

a.

b.
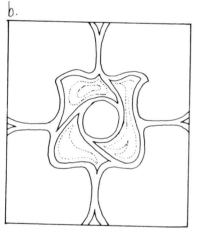

c.

d.

e.

f.
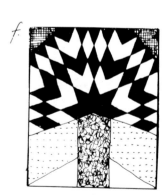

g.

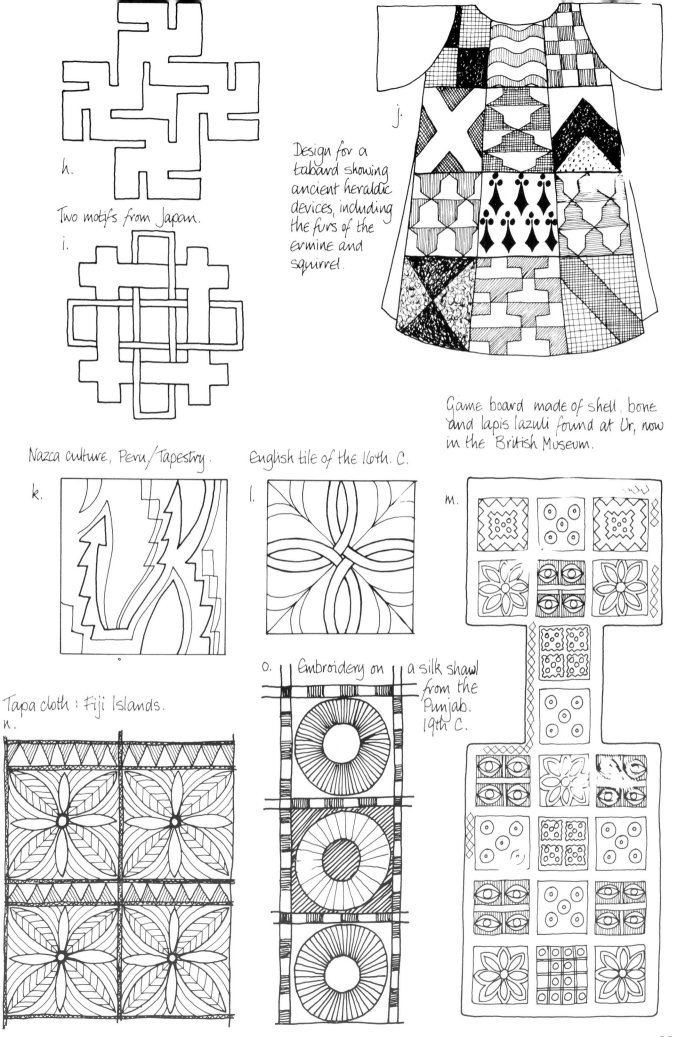

h.

Two motifs from Japan.

i.

Design for a tabard showing ancient heraldic devices, including the furs of the ermine and squirrel.

j.

Game board made of shell, bone and lapis lazuli found at Ur, now in the British Museum.

Nazca culture, Peru./Tapestry.

k.

English tile of the 16th. C.

l.

m.

Tapa cloth : Fiji Islands.

n.

o. Embroidery on a silk shawl from the Punjab. 19th C.

a.

b. Earth symbol. In India, it means good luck.

c.

d.

Triangles

a. f. g. h. and i.   Quilt blocks used both in America and England.

c. Pueblo Indian motif from a pottery vessel.

d. and I. Taaniko weaving designs: New Zealand.

e. The letters A. K. M. N. V. W. X. Y. Z all have triangles in their capital forms. Patterns can be made with these.

j. and k. Gustav Klimpt (1862-1918) used triangles in a free-form construction on the robe of this highly-stylized figure. She is set against a background of swirling golden spirals, which are repeated inside some of the triangles. Collectively, they emphasise the triangular shape of the standing figure.

As half-squares and half-diamonds, triangles are one of the most versatile pattern shapes and have always been popular with designers since earliest times.

f.

e.

g.

h.

i.

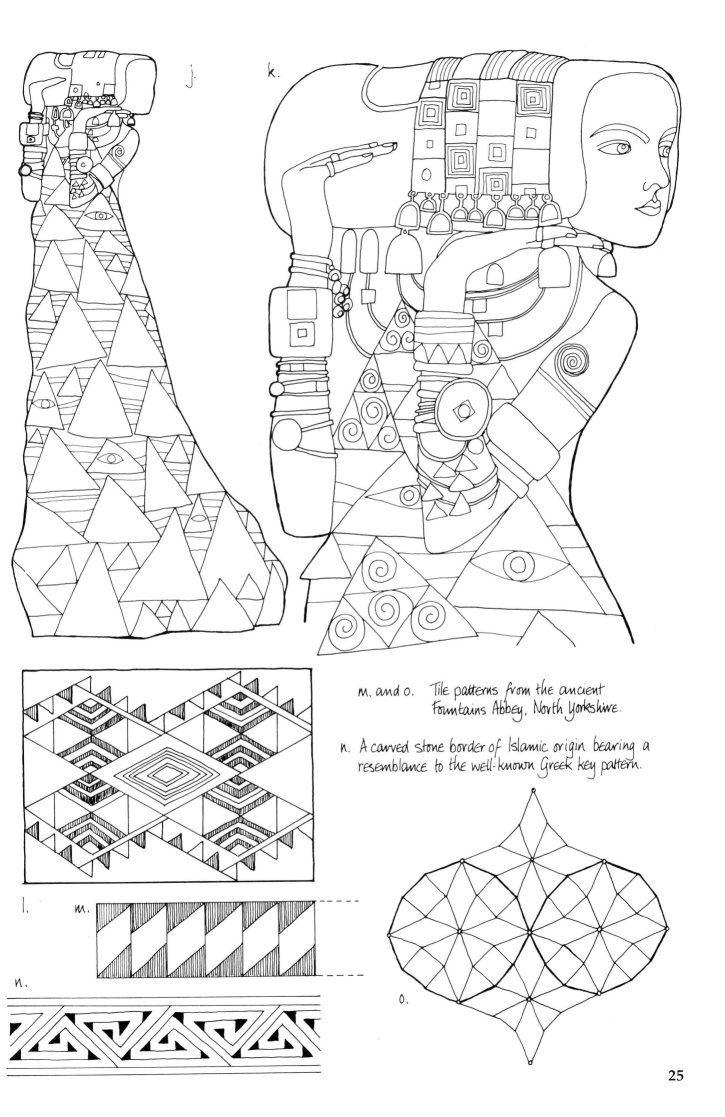

j.

k.

m. and o. Tile patterns from the ancient
Fountains Abbey, North Yorkshire.

n. A carved stone border of Islamic origin bearing a
resemblance to the well-known Greek key pattern.

l.

m.

n.

o.

Circles

The circle is the universal symbol, used since men began to make marks on cave walls, to symbolize the sun, moon, earth, the self and eternity. Examples are not hard to find or to invent: the ones shown here are from a wide variety of sources and eras and some are mere "doodles", but the natural world offers as many ideas as the man-made. Look up any of the following sources:

Microscopic organisms, snowflakes, etc.
Sea urchins and starfish
Flowers, fruit and vegetable cross sections
Pebbles and marbles and paperweights
Vases, plates and other ceramics
Clock faces, wheels and engine parts
Brooches, rings and neck ornaments
Circular windows and
　　　　　other architetural features
Baskets and buttons
Carpets and rugs
Medallions and decorative symbols

All the examples here have been drawn free-hand. The rather inexact effect is, I feel, more attractive than the too-precise "engine-turned" circle produced by a compass, and practise soon produces adequate results.

Nature abounds with examples of radiating lines, particularly in foliage. The small drawing is a design by the Spanish architect Antoni Gaudi (1852-1926) for part of a wrought iron gate based on palm fronds, seen above.

Snowflake patterns are always based on six points.

Below: within the circle, a tracing of the centre of this brassica shows freely radiating lines. A second

draft would eliminate the leaves and continue all lines to the edges of the circle. The negative spaces (between the lines) are as interesting as the positive ones.

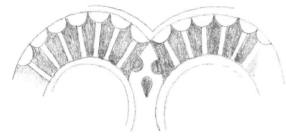

Connecting Circles

Take time to analyse complex patterns like this mosaic (in a large basin now in the Victoria and Albert Museum, London) and you will find that various elements can be used in isolation, like the ones in the sketch above.

Tile patterns too appear complex at first glance, but study will show that many consist of quite simple repeated elements. It is often the variation in colours which gives the impression of complexity.

Early 14th century tile. English.

Tiles from Rievaulx Abbey, North Yorkshire.

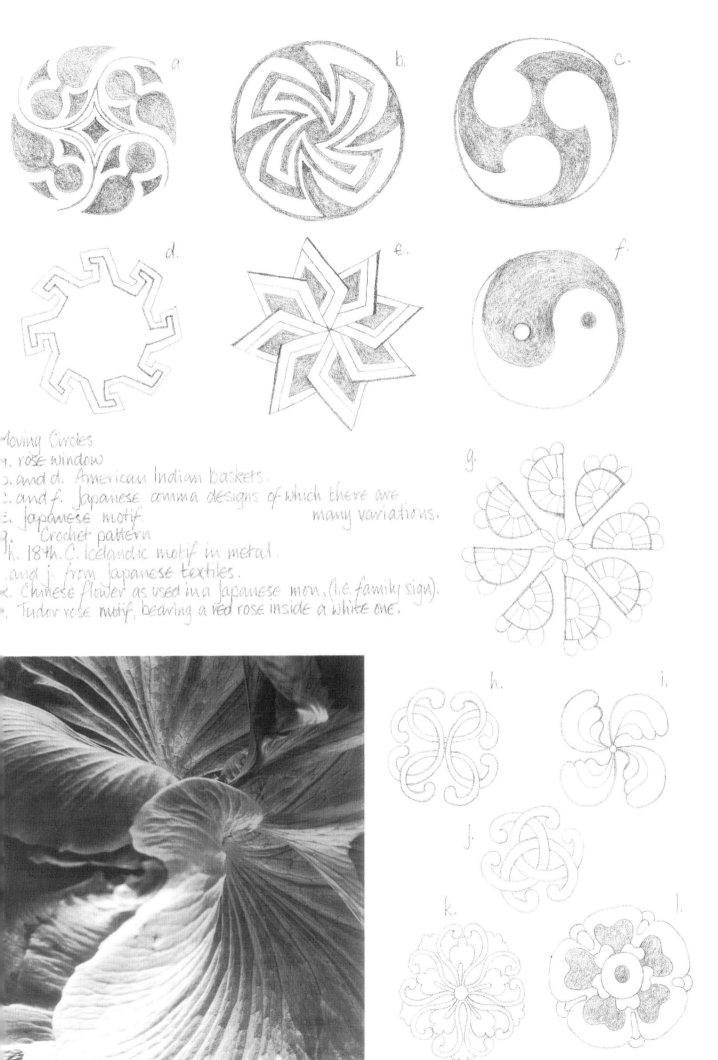

Moving Circles

a. rose window

b. and d. American Indian baskets.

c. and f. Japanese comma designs of which there are many variations.

e. Japanese motif.

g. Crochet pattern

h. 18th. C. Icelandic motif in metal.

i. and j. from Japanese textiles.

k. Chinese flower as used in a Japanese mon, (i.e family sign).

l. Tudor rose motif, bearing a red rose inside a white one.

Spirals

snail

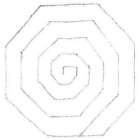

William de Morgan tile

19th C. white cotton knitted spirals

Below: pattern of spirals from the oldest known quilt in the world dating from between 100 B.C. — 200 A.D. from the tomb of a Scythian chieftain.

Above: spiral staircase in the tropical glass house at Kew showing a mass of intricate patterns.

More spiral patterns can be seen in sea-shells, octopus tentacles, animal-horns, coiled + curled-up animals, spiral-growing plants, e.g. fern fronds, ropes, spiral-spun yarns + whirlwinds.

Below: a pattern of spirals and chevrons on a neolithic Japanese vase of the first millenium B.C. (National Museum, Tokyo)

Triple spiral motif, possibly a symbol of birth, death and rebirth, seen on the west side-chamber of the passage-grave at New Grange, County Meath, Ireland, c. 2500 B.C.

Ceiling design Greek : Pre - 1104 B.C.

Persian ornament on the floor of the stairs in the palace of Artaxerxes.

Chilean pot decoration.

Right and below: Greek prehistoric ornament

Spiral motifs on the back neck (left) and front panel (above) from two 18th C. peasant smocks

Above: lower edge of an Imperial Chinese hunting robe. K'ang Hsi (1662-1722) V. & A. Museum

Interlinking spiral border, Peruvian 14th - 15th C.

Below right: incised design of spirals on a pot from Arkansas

Right: painted design on a pot from Mississippi

Like the circle, the spiral has always held a deep symbolic significance and examples of its various forms can be found world-wide from pre-historic to present times.
See "Embroidered Textiles" by Sheila Paine ISBN 0 500 23597 X and "An Illustrated Encyclopaedia of Traditional Symbols" by J.C. Cooper ISBN 0 500 27125 9

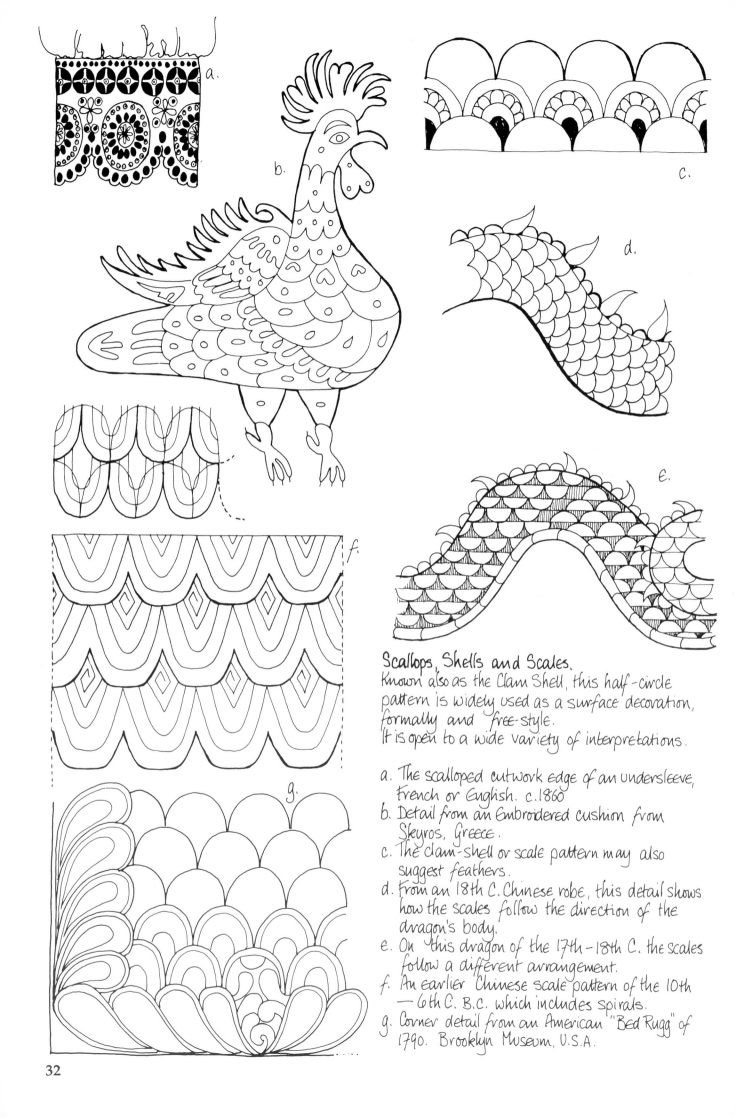

a.

b.

c.

d.

e.

f.

g.

Scallops, Shells and Scales.

Known also as the Clam Shell, this half-circle pattern is widely used as a surface decoration, formally and free-style.
It is open to a wide variety of interpretations.

a. The scalloped cutwork edge of an undersleeve, French or English. c.1860

b. Detail from an Embroidered cushion from Skyros, Greece.

c. The clam-shell or scale pattern may also suggest feathers.

d. From an 18th C. Chinese robe, this detail shows how the scales follow the direction of the dragon's body.

e. On this dragon of the 17th - 18th C. the scales follow a different arrangement.

f. An earlier Chinese scale pattern of the 10th — 6th C. B.C. which includes spirals.

g. Corner detail from an American "Bed Rugg" of 1790. Brooklyn Museum, U.S.A.

Animal patterns

a. Japanese crane motif
b. Glazed ceramic motif — 13th-14th C.
c. Border of camels from a 19th C.
   kilim from W. Africa. V. & A. Museum.
d. Left-half of a symmetrical ikat
   design of deer and tiny creatures
   from Indonesia.
e. 6th C. Coptic tapestry panel in the
   Burrell Collection, Glasgow, showing a
   small animal surrounded by vine leaves.
f. Detail from a pattern, in blue and white
   chequered squares, of fearsome monsters.
   The fur and feather patterns are worth noting.
   Middle Sweden. 15th C.
g. Detail from the centre of a Chilkat shirt
   representing the brown bear.

33

a. circular flower motif

b. and c. traditional quilting designs

a.

b.

c.

d. detail from a Baltimore quilt of 1847.

d.

e. geometric patchwork motif.

e.

h. "Bird and Leaf" design by C.F.A.Voysey. c. 1905

f.

f. Detail from a Persian brocaded silk of the 17th C.

g. Ojibway beadwork pattern

g.

h.

34

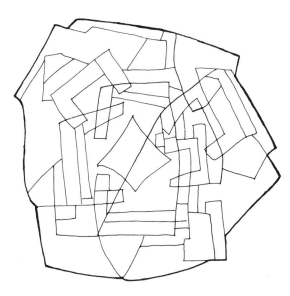

Flowers and Foliage

This intricate design is only one of many from the extensive portfolio of Edouard Benedictus (d.1930), one of the outstanding artists of the Art Deco movement. Bold, geometric lines intersect the flowers and foliage to create a rhythm of tones which appear as a patchwork of interlocking shapes. A tiny area has been shaded to explain how these are distributed. Two points particularly are worth noting; one is the way in which the centre of the flowers is emphasised by concentric lines while those on the leaves spring from base to tip. Also note the ragged edge of the border inside the frame as though tissue paper had been torn away all round. Indeed, many of his patterns give the impression of a tissue-paper construction, while his colour-combinations alone are worth studying. Benedictus' "Art Deco Designs in Colour" is published by Dover. ISBN 0·486·23971·3

a.

b.

a. Hand-made and painted tile with blue leaves and orange fruit, made by J. van Hulst, Harlingen, Holland. c. 1885

Both a. and b. are examples of pattern made only by the outer shapes of the leaves and flowers.

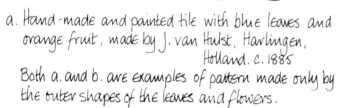

b. Cherry blossom pattern, Japanese textile.
c. Tibetan rug with a pattern of stylized chrysanthemums with an inner border of wave patterns known as "still water".
d. This well-known stylized flower border of inter-twined stems can be seen on many embroidered samplers of the 17th and 18th centuries.

c.

In c. and d. more details imply the use of a greater range of colours and textures. This is borne out by the techniques used.

d.

Foliage Borders

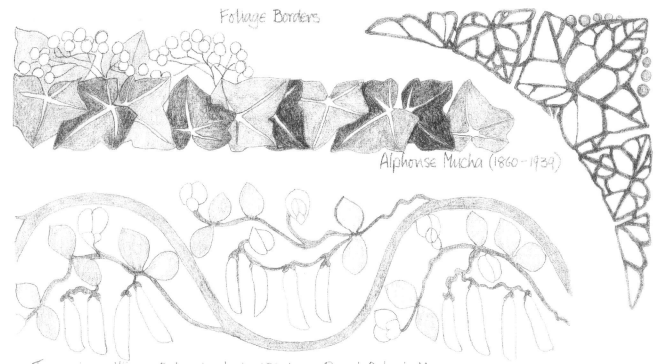

Alphonse Mucha (1860-1939)

Trapunto quilting, Ontario. Late 1860's   Royal Ontario Museum

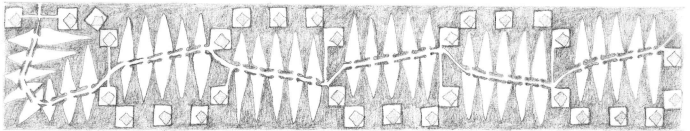

Koloman Moser (1868-1916)   Book illustration detail

"Buttercup"   E.A.Seguy (Art Nouveau period)

Simplified drawing of 19th C. Honiton Lace   V.+ A. Museum

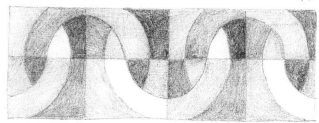

a.

b.

Borders

Border patterns differ from all-over patterns only in formation. They follow a line, usually around the edge of something (plain or patterned) and may be wide, narrow, straight, curved, short or continuous. The width of a border should bear a direct relationship to the rest of the design and this will usually be decided by the combination of eye and experience rather than by mathematical formula. A wide and brightly coloured border pattern will overwhelm a delicate design of pastel tones placed next to it, and vice-versa, so care must be taken to see one as an extension of the other. In other words, the border should always be in keeping with the rest of the design in terms of style, scale, weight and colour. Quite often, an element from the main design can be borrowed to become a repeating motif in the border, thus creating an overall unity. Note how often this has been done wherever you see an attractive border on wallpaper, fabric or wood carving and see how the border becomes a natural progression of the rest of the design, even where this is only a colour or texture.

c.

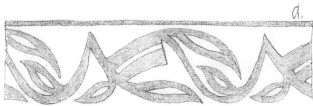

d.

a. Benedictus. Art Deco period.

b. Ancient stamp from Mexico.

c. and d. Pueblo pottery designs from New Mexico.

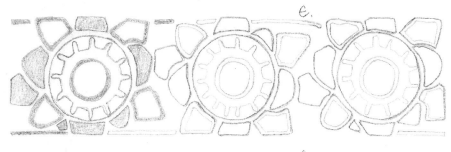

e.

e. Seguy. Art Nouveau period.

f.

f. Ancient cylindrical stamp from Mexico City.

g.

g. German woodcut of 1533 seen here without the calligraphy on the band.